To the MAN who I let HURT me for way to long...IM STRONGER than you thought!

Don't be a fool for too long. When you realize you're being taken for granite it's time to make moves. Life isn't meant to be lived in settling for less than you deserve.

You can't expect something different from someone who hasn't done anything to change. Don't stunt your growth waiting on someone else who doesn't want to grow.

If you don't feel worthy it will show in every aspect of your life. People will give you only what you feel you deserve! Set the bar I don't compromise.

Don't cry over someone that doesn't cry over you. Don't hold on to Someone that's not holding onto you. You don't have to hate them, but you can love them from a distance.

Negative people need drama like oxygen! Stay positive! It'll take their breath away!

Shady people will expose themselves. Don't disrupt your happiness by trying to be Sherlock Holmes. Just sit back and pay attention. The truth will surface!

True love should never have to be hid. If you're a secret and you're probably just an option not a priority.

Don't fall in love with the idea of love if there is no real love. A lot of people are in loveless relationship but afraid to leave because they've fallen in love with the idea. Don't get it twisted. It's either real love or it isn't. Don't be afraid to let go of the idea so you can create the reality.

Stop praising boyfriends… Until a man wants a woman down the aisle, he's just auditioning. Don't give a boyfriend the benefit of a husband. No the difference between dating and marriage so every Tom, Dick, and Harry can't say they all had all of you.

How many chances… Do you give someone who's not making any changes. Their mouth keeps saying one thing but their actions are saying something different. You have to forgive them for wasting your time and move on!

The problem wasn't him, it was you. You made excuses for his bad behavior, you excepted his obvious lies, and you gave him another chance, again and again. You sold yourself short, you didn't believe you deserve better, and you stay too long. You learn the hard way... But you know what you still learned.

When faced with two choices, simply toss a coin. It works not because it settles the question for you but because in that brief moment when the coins in the air, you suddenly know what you were hoping for.

I never argue with people anymore. I don't vibrate at that level, if you want to fight I'll let you do it with yourself. If you want war, fight yourself. I run from abusive people and interactions. I deserve love over hate and peace more than war.

Neither time changes nor do people… The only thing that changes what time is our perceptions and our priorities.

Don't give a man more than he gives you. If you respect you, respect him! If he loves you, love him! If he promotes you to the world, promote him! But if you're a secret that he miss treats, he needs to become a piece of your history.

A woman can always tell if a Man loves her by how much time he's willing to invest. Money spent is meaningless, but time spent is priceless.

You have to love yourself enough to Set a standard for your life that you're unwilling to compromise. If you except the standards of others for your life you'll never be happy.

I found out along time ago... That true love isn't a fight... You don't have to for something that's meant to be... You don't have to beg someone to stay if they really love you... If the love is mutual there is no struggle... True love is effortless when both parties buy in... Stop fighting, start loving!

Treat your relationship like your house... Build on a firm foundation... Pay your dues... Keep your grass cut so you can see those snakes... Lock your doors to keep strangers out... And always bring something to the table...

Love is selfless. Love is give-and-take. Love is a two-way street. If what you're getting is it being reciprocated, you're not being loved, you're being used.

You have to be willing to lose them to keep them. If they feel like you'll stay no matter what, they will never respect you. But as soon as they realize that you're strong enough to live without them, that's when they see your true value.

Don't play with fire. You'll get a small hints from a person that lets you know they might burn you. Trust your intuition, it's rarely wrong!

It's not about what you buy her it's about how you treat her faithfulness honesty and love matters most!

You can't let everyone speak into your life because some people don't know their left from the right and want to give you directions. Not everybody cares, some people just want to hear your problems to feel better about their life.

Strong women are not attracted to weak men.Strong men are not attracted to weak women. You may not always want to believe it, but you are a reflection of who you put up with. Choose wisely.

If someone is taking you for granted , their access must no longer be granted. Time is too precious to waste on someone that doesn't value your time. Sometimes loving yourself means letting someone else to go.

People put too much emphasis on toughing it out and putting up with all the bull... A relationship shouldn't be a fight. It shouldn't be a struggle.If both people are actually committed to one another, it's not hard at all.

True love removes all insecurities. If you are in secure in your relationship, that's a clear sign that some love is missing. Love with everything or let it go.

You can't keep crying and not taking action. Arguing and crying won't change anything. Set standards, lead with love, and if your love isn't reciprocated it's time to make changes!

Walk away if he chooses to love you only behind closed doors.

When your tears out number your smiles, it's time to make some changes. The pain won't change until you make changes.

Don't hurt the one you claim
to love while trying to entertain
the one who isn't worthy of
your love.

You have to help yourself
before you can help someone
else. Start loving yourself
more and everything else will
flow from there.

We have to stop start making excuses for adults. If they don't want to grow then let them go. If they only get three strikes in the game then why would you give them more than that in real life? Don't talk yourself out of what you deserve.

Don't confuse standards with preferences. Standards are things you need in a partner. Preferences or things you want in a partner. Sometimes what you want isn't what you need. Recognize when that's the case.

Stop settling… You don't have to lay on your back to get a man… You don't have to compete with another woman to keep a man… You don't have to turn yourself into bait to catch a mate… You don't have to settle for half a man… Stop settling!!

Don't quit on love, if love hasn't quit on you. Relationships fail because someone stops giving their all. Love is a job you can't retire from. You have to show up every day and bring your best effort. Keep doing the things you did to fall in love, and you won't have to worry about falling out of love. Don't quit on love !

Do you have real friends, or do you have glorified associates? Be careful who you call a friend! Just because you're a good friend doesn't mean that everyone in your circle will be a good friend to you. Choose your friends wisely!

Everybody needs you, but you
need you first. Don't help
everyone else and not
yourself. Love your neighbor
as you love yourself, not
instead of yourself.

Wake up feeling blessed! Your
thoughts will determine the
quality of your life. Don't give
into the worries of the world.
Trust God and walk by faith.

The enemy is busy. There will be a test everywhere you turn. Stay prayed up. They ready. Overcome every obstacle with prayer and Positivity. If you start losing in your mind, you'll lose in life.

When we would cheat on a test in school it was because we were dumb to the subject, lazy, and untrustworthy, or we did not respect our teacher… Those are the same reasons we cheat in a relationship. Dumb, lazy, and untrustworthy, and we don't respect our partner don't get it twisted, cheating is ruthless!

If you can't focus and enjoy your days work because someone is running through your mind for all the wrong reasons, it's time to reconsider that relationship. Love brings peace not pain.

Self-love it doesn't mean that everyone will treat you the way you deserve to be treated. It means that you won't let them change the way you see yourself, nor will you stick around for them to destroy you.

A real woman is worthy… She brings stability to a man's life… She brings favor from the Lord… No amount of money or fame can replace her… Her quality outweighs quantity… She is the backbone and support to the body… She's the CEO of the household she's enough for a real man… God showed unfair favor when he made her!

A woman is worth more than just sex. Make time to truly get to know her as a person, and connect with her on a deeper level.

Your time is limited so don't waste it living someone else's life. Don't be trapped by dogma which is living the results of other people's thinking. Don't let the noise of other's opinions drown out your own Inner voice. And most importantly, have the Courage to follow your heart and into Wisdom. They somehow already know what you truly want to become. Everything else is secondary.

You can't carry able-bodied adults to your mountain top. They will weigh you down and eventually bring you down. If they are unwilling to climb, let them watch. Pray the best for them and leave them in gods hands.

Be all in or get out! Nothing is worse than being in a relationship, friendship, or partnership with people who are half in and half out. Be all in or nothing at all!

Don't get by! There's a lot of women on a rent to own plan with their man. Don't ignore the red flags for some red bottoms. Just because a man buys nice gifts doesn't mean he's a good man. Evaluate his character and let that be his Currency.

Do you really love yourself ? You're telling yourself that you do. What are your actions saying ? Are you settling for less than you deserve ? Are you still putting up with the same stuff you were putting up with this time last month or last year ? If you know when your heart is time to walk away, then why stay ?

Don't stand still. If they want to be with you, they will catch up. Don't wait on a person because they may never come around and you won't ever get your time back. Live your life and if they want to be in it they will make the necessary adjustments.

Ladies hear this if a man isn't following God, he isn't fit to lead… And if he doesn't have a relationship with God he won't know how to have a relationship with you… If he doesn't know God, he doesn't know real love…

Don't be a cheater… You're the one losing in life if you think you're playing the game and winning but you're actually losing. You can get over on some people, but you can't fool your creator. You will reap what you sow, so you better start trying to grow. Juggling relationships between different people doesn't make you cool, eventually it'll make you look like a clown.

People don't cheat by chance, they cheat by choice. It's never an accident because They've played it out in their mind before it happened. Be very careful if you stay with someone who has cheated on you without reason. What you except is all you will ever get.

Respect your body. Keep your private parts for your private partner. Only perverted grown boys want to see you half naked online. It's a cold world. Keep your clothes on!

When did violence become a part of love? A person doesn't abuse you because they love you. That person abuses you because they hate themselves and are incapable of truly loving you. Don't get it twisted. Abuse isn't love!!

Don't be a victim of someone else's pain. Some people are hurting so bad they don't know how to love. Love them, but no when you need to love from a distance. A person has to want to heal for you to help them heal.

Stop looking back… If a person chose to step out of your life, leave them there! Not everyone who started with you will finish with you. Be OKAY with that!

Don't allow yourself to ignore the warning signs. People who don't care for your heart or your time will want you to remain blind to the signs. If you see them, run. Life is too fragile to let someone waste your time and your love.

Do not worry about Tricks and Cheats. If some people are trying to trap and hurt you, that is ok because GOD is also trapping them. Hole digger's fall in their holes. No bad remain non-punished, no good remains non rewarded. Remain Happy and then let justice take course.

I told you I'd move on. I told you I'd let you go Someday Honestly, It was the hardest thing I've ever done but it was worth it. For me, for my heart. You Hurt me so bad. You killed my trust, you changed me. I knew I could be strong enough to let you go. I knew it and I did it. I can't explain how proud I am. Because the only one who knows how much you hurt me is me. But here I am now, healing. We may love the wrong person, cry for the wrong person, but one thing is for sure, mistakes will help us find the right person someday.

Just learn from your mistakes.

My life. My choices. My mistakes. My lessons. Not your business. Finally taken charge of my life I am a survivor.

Cheating isn't always kissing, touching, or flirting. If you got to delete text messages so your partner won't see them, you're already there.

Instead of wiping away your tears wipe away the people who made you cry.

Respect yourself enough to walk away from anyone or anything that no longer serves you, grows you, or makes you happy.

She promised herself better
and never looked back!!!

Never hurt people who love
you a lot, because they won't
hurt you back. But they'll
probably have no choice but
to leave you forever.

Made in the USA
Monee, IL
07 July 2026

56552412R00033